Just For Today
12 weeks

Left-Handed Edition

www.gratitudeandmore.ca

Copyright © 2016 by Leah Strange

All rights reserved.

This book may not be re-sold. No part of this book may be used, reproduced or transmitted by any means without written permission by the author.

Left-Handed Edition: *Although there is writing to do on both sides of the page, the lined pages for additional notes have been moved to the left-hand side. We have also found that many right-handed people prefer this layout.*

This journal was created with the intention of helping those in recovery with their daily inventory. It is by no means a complete checklist, but my hope is that it will assist with spot check inventories taken at any time of the day.

Each day has two pages, one with daily prompts and one lined page for any additional writing. There is also a Weekly Check-In page that allows you to review the previous week and set your intention for the coming days.

The purpose of the daily questions is to allow you to reach deep into yourself and discover the place where the answers are—but usually remain hidden. Only those brave enough to begin the excavation will reap the rewards.

Finally, the back pages are there for you to fill in any new contact information. I hope you enjoy your journey over the next twelve weeks.

For more information on the wide variety of journals we offer, visit us at www.gratitudeandmore.ca

I wish you luck on your journey. Stay open.

Leah

WEEKLY CHECK-IN

My Intention for Next Week:

I would like to:

Experience...

Let go of...

Feel...

Learn to...

Stop...

I want more of...	I want less of...

The most effective way to do it, is to do it. (Amelia Earhart)

Date:	Mood/Happiness Scale (1-10): AM PM
I am grateful for:	
What is happening in my life today?	

Was I of service?	Did I share how I was feeling?
I'm excited about:	Did I enrich my spiritual life?
What am I fearful of?	Do I owe an amend?
Did I struggle today?	Why?
Was I kind?	My plan for tomorrow:
Was I Hungry, Angry, Lonely or Tired?	

I am comfortable in my body and all is well.

Date:	Mood/Happiness Scale (1-10): AM PM
I am grateful for:	
What is happening in my life today?	
Was I of service?	Did I share how I was feeling?
I'm excited about:	Did I enrich my spiritual life?
What am I fearful of?	Do I owe an amend?
Did I struggle today?	Why?
Was I kind?	My plan for tomorrow:
Was I Hungry, Angry, Lonely or Tired?	

Ruach: An explosive, expansive, surprising, creative energy that surges through all things. (Ancient Hebrew)

Date:	Mood/Happiness Scale (1-10): AM PM
I am grateful for:	
What is happening in my life today?	
Was I of service?	Did I share how I was feeling?
I'm excited about:	Did I enrich my spiritual life?
What am I fearful of?	Do I owe an amend?
Did I struggle today?	Why?
Was I kind?	My plan for tomorrow:
Was I Hungry, Angry, Lonely or Tired?	

To thine own self be true. (William Shakespeare)

Date:	Mood/Happiness Scale (1-10): AM PM
I am grateful for:	
What is happening in my life today?	
Was I of service?	Did I share how I was feeling?
I'm excited about:	Did I enrich my spiritual life?
What am I fearful of?	Do I owe an amend?
Did I struggle today?	Why?
Was I kind?	My plan for tomorrow:
Was I Hungry, Angry, Lonely or Tired?	

Dare to be remarkable!

Date:	Mood/Happiness Scale (1-10): AM PM
I am grateful for:	
What is happening in my life today?	

Was I of service?	Did I share how I was feeling?
I'm excited about:	Did I enrich my spiritual life?
What am I fearful of?	Do I owe an amend?
Did I struggle today?	Why?
Was I kind?	My plan for tomorrow:
Was I Hungry, Angry, Lonely or Tired?	

Abundance flows through me. I am a channel for the Universe.

Date:	Mood/Happiness Scale (1-10): AM PM
I am grateful for:	

What is happening in my life today?

Was I of service?	Did I share how I was feeling?
I'm excited about:	Did I enrich my spiritual life?
What am I fearful of?	Do I owe an amend?
Did I struggle today?	Why?
Was I kind?	My plan for tomorrow:
Was I Hungry, Angry, Lonely or Tired?	

Rise! Do not shrink.

Date:	Mood/Happiness Scale (1-10): AM PM

I am grateful for:

What is happening in my life today?

Was I of service?	Did I share how I was feeling?
I'm excited about:	Did I enrich my spiritual life?
What am I fearful of?	Do I owe an amend?
Did I struggle today?	Why?
Was I kind?	My plan for tomorrow:
Was I Hungry, Angry, Lonely or Tired?	

REVIEW OF LAST WEEK

How balanced was my time? (work/family/Me)	Did I get outside every day for fresh air?
Did I have the support I needed?	Did I ask for help when I needed it?

Did I remember my intentions from last week?

Did I spend enough time being unplugged?

I am proud that I....

Notes:

WEEKLY CHECK-IN

My Intention for Next Week:

I would like to:

Experience...

Let go of...

Feel...

Learn to...

Stop...

I want more of...	I want less of...

You are worthy. You are important. You are loved.

Date:	Mood/Happiness Scale (1-10): AM PM
I am grateful for:	
What is happening in my life today?	

Was I of service?	Did I share how I was feeling?
I'm excited about:	Did I enrich my spiritual life?
What am I fearful of?	Do I owe an amend?
Did I struggle today?	Why?
Was I kind?	My plan for tomorrow:
Was I Hungry, Angry, Lonely or Tired?	

The Universe is conspiring with you, never against you.

Date:	Mood/Happiness Scale (1-10): AM PM

I am grateful for:

What is happening in my life today?

Was I of service?	Did I share how I was feeling?
I'm excited about:	Did I enrich my spiritual life?
What am I fearful of?	Do I owe an amend?
Did I struggle today?	Why?
Was I kind?	My plan for tomorrow:
Was I Hungry, Angry, Lonely or Tired?	

All that I seek is already within me.

Date:	Mood/Happiness Scale (1-10): AM PM
I am grateful for:	
What is happening in my life today?	

Was I of service?	Did I share how I was feeling?
I'm excited about:	Did I enrich my spiritual life?
What am I fearful of?	Do I owe an amend?
Did I struggle today?	Why?
Was I kind?	My plan for tomorrow:
Was I Hungry, Angry, Lonely or Tired?	

I am guided by my intention. I am open to the Universe.

Date:	Mood/Happiness Scale (1-10): AM PM
I am grateful for:	
What is happening in my life today?	

Was I of service?	Did I share how I was feeling?
I'm excited about:	Did I enrich my spiritual life?
What am I fearful of?	Do I owe an amend?
Did I struggle today?	Why?
Was I kind?	My plan for tomorrow:
Was I Hungry, Angry, Lonely or Tired?	

I am unlimited. My life is filled with abundance.

Date:	Mood/Happiness Scale (1-10): AM PM
I am grateful for:	
What is happening in my life today?	
Was I of service?	Did I share how I was feeling?
I'm excited about:	Did I enrich my spiritual life?
What am I fearful of?	Do I owe an amend?
Did I struggle today?	Why?
Was I kind?	My plan for tomorrow:
Was I Hungry, Angry, Lonely or Tired?	

I have freed myself from fear and self-doubt.

Date:	Mood/Happiness Scale (1-10): AM PM

I am grateful for:

What is happening in my life today?

Was I of service?	Did I share how I was feeling?
I'm excited about:	Did I enrich my spiritual life?
What am I fearful of?	Do I owe an amend?
Did I struggle today?	Why?
Was I kind?	My plan for tomorrow:
Was I Hungry, Angry, Lonely or Tired?	

I am in sync. I flow with the river of life.

Date:	Mood/Happiness Scale (1-10): AM PM
I am grateful for:	
What is happening in my life today?	
Was I of service?	Did I share how I was feeling?
I'm excited about:	Did I enrich my spiritual life?
What am I fearful of?	Do I owe an amend?
Did I struggle today?	Why?
Was I kind?	My plan for tomorrow:
Was I Hungry, Angry, Lonely or Tired?	

REVIEW OF LAST WEEK

How balanced was my time? (work/family/Me)	Did I get outside every day for fresh air?
Did I have the support I needed?	Did I ask for help when I needed it?

Did I remember my intentions from last week?

Did I spend enough time being unplugged?

I am proud that I....

Notes:

WEEKLY CHECK-IN

My Intention for Next Week:

I would like to:

Experience...

Let go of...

Feel...

Learn to...

Stop...

I want more of...	I want less of...

I choose to release fear, anger, hurt and resentment.

Date:	Mood/Happiness Scale (1-10): AM　　　　　　　PM
I am grateful for:			

What is happening in my life today?

Was I of service?	Did I share how I was feeling?
I'm excited about:	Did I enrich my spiritual life?
What am I fearful of?	Do I owe an amend?
Did I struggle today?	Why?
Was I kind?	My plan for tomorrow:
Was I Hungry, Angry, Lonely or Tired?	

I forgive others; I love myself and deserve the freedom it brings.

Date:	Mood/Happiness Scale (1-10): AM 　　　　　　 PM
I am grateful for:	
What is happening in my life today?	

Was I of service?	Did I share how I was feeling?
I'm excited about:	Did I enrich my spiritual life?
What am I fearful of?	Do I owe an amend?
Did I struggle today?	Why?
Was I kind?	My plan for tomorrow:
Was I Hungry, Angry, Lonely or Tired?	

How do you act authentically?

Date:	Mood/Happiness Scale (1-10): AM PM
I am grateful for:	
What is happening in my life today?	
Was I of service?	Did I share how I was feeling?
I'm excited about:	Did I enrich my spiritual life?
What am I fearful of?	Do I owe an amend?
Did I struggle today?	Why?
Was I kind?	My plan for tomorrow:
Was I Hungry, Angry, Lonely or Tired?	

I am open to new experiences and new people.

Date:	Mood/Happiness Scale (1-10): AM PM

I am grateful for:

What is happening in my life today?

Was I of service?	Did I share how I was feeling?
I'm excited about:	Did I enrich my spiritual life?
What am I fearful of?	Do I owe an amend?

Did I struggle today?	Why?

Was I kind?	My plan for tomorrow:
Was I Hungry, Angry, Lonely or Tired?	

Be still and know that I am God. (Psalm 46:10)

Date:	Mood/Happiness Scale (1-10): AM PM

I am grateful for:

What is happening in my life today?

Was I of service?	Did I share how I was feeling?
I'm excited about:	Did I enrich my spiritual life?
What am I fearful of?	Do I owe an amend?
Did I struggle today?	Why?
Was I kind?	My plan for tomorrow:
Was I Hungry, Angry, Lonely or Tired?	

I am patient, tolerant and filled with compassion.

Date:	Mood/Happiness Scale (1-10): AM PM
I am grateful for:	
What is happening in my life today?	

Was I of service?	Did I share how I was feeling?
I'm excited about:	Did I enrich my spiritual life?
What am I fearful of?	Do I owe an amend?
Did I struggle today?	Why?
Was I kind?	My plan for tomorrow:
Was I Hungry, Angry, Lonely or Tired?	

I love every cell of my beautiful self.

Date:	Mood/Happiness Scale (1-10): AM PM
I am grateful for:	
What is happening in my life today?	
Was I of service?	Did I share how I was feeling?
I'm excited about:	Did I enrich my spiritual life?
What am I fearful of?	Do I owe an amend?
Did I struggle today?	Why?
Was I kind?	My plan for tomorrow:
Was I Hungry, Angry, Lonely or Tired?	

REVIEW OF LAST WEEK

How balanced was my time? (work/family/Me)	Did I get outside every day for fresh air?
Did I have the support I needed?	Did I ask for help when I needed it?

Did I remember my intentions from last week?

Did I spend enough time being unplugged?

I am proud that I....

Notes:

WEEKLY CHECK-IN

My Intention for Next Week:

I would like to:

Experience...

Let go of...

Feel...

Learn to...

Stop...

I want more of...	I want less of...

I am protected and safe.

Date:	Mood/Happiness Scale (1-10): AM　　　　　　　　PM
I am grateful for:	
What is happening in my life today?	
Was I of service?	Did I share how I was feeling?
I'm excited about:	Did I enrich my spiritual life?
What am I fearful of?	Do I owe an amend?
Did I struggle today?	Why?
Was I kind?	My plan for tomorrow:
Was I Hungry, Angry, Lonely or Tired?	

My body is strong and supports me in all I do.

Date:	Mood/Happiness Scale (1-10): AM PM
I am grateful for:	
What is happening in my life today?	

Was I of service?	Did I share how I was feeling?
I'm excited about:	Did I enrich my spiritual life?
What am I fearful of?	Do I owe an amend?
Did I struggle today?	Why?
Was I kind?	My plan for tomorrow:
Was I Hungry, Angry, Lonely or Tired?	

My life is unfolding with ease.

Date:	Mood/Happiness Scale (1-10): AM PM

I am grateful for:

What is happening in my life today?

Was I of service?	Did I share how I was feeling?
I'm excited about:	Did I enrich my spiritual life?
What am I fearful of?	Do I owe an amend?
Did I struggle today?	Why?
Was I kind? Was I Hungry, Angry, Lonely or Tired?	My plan for tomorrow:

My days are filled with excitement and love.

Date:	Mood/Happiness Scale (1-10): AM PM
I am grateful for:	
What is happening in my life today?	
Was I of service?	Did I share how I was feeling?
I'm excited about:	Did I enrich my spiritual life?
What am I fearful of?	Do I owe an amend?
Did I struggle today?	Why?
Was I kind?	My plan for tomorrow:
Was I Hungry, Angry, Lonely or Tired?	

Serenity is not the absence of conflict, but the ability to cope with it.

Date:	Mood/Happiness Scale (1-10): AM　　　　　　PM
I am grateful for:			

What is happening in my life today?

Was I of service?	Did I share how I was feeling?
I'm excited about:	Did I enrich my spiritual life?
What am I fearful of?	Do I owe an amend?
Did I struggle today?	Why?
Was I kind?	My plan for tomorrow:
Was I Hungry, Angry, Lonely or Tired?	

At the center of your being you have the answer; you know who you are and you know what you want. (Lao Tzu)

Date:	Mood/Happiness Scale (1-10): AM PM

I am grateful for:

What is happening in my life today?

Was I of service?	Did I share how I was feeling?
I'm excited about:	Did I enrich my spiritual life?
What am I fearful of?	Do I owe an amend?
Did I struggle today?	Why?
Was I kind?	My plan for tomorrow:
Was I Hungry, Angry, Lonely or Tired?	

Everyone has a story. It's not how you tell it. It's how you live it.

Date:	Mood/Happiness Scale (1-10): AM　　　　　　　　PM
I am grateful for:	
What is happening in my life today?	

Was I of service?	Did I share how I was feeling?
I'm excited about:	Did I enrich my spiritual life?
What am I fearful of?	Do I owe an amend?
Did I struggle today?	Why?
Was I kind?	My plan for tomorrow:
Was I Hungry, Angry, Lonely or Tired?	

REVIEW OF LAST WEEK

How balanced was my time? (work/family/Me)	Did I get outside every day for fresh air?
Did I have the support I needed?	Did I ask for help when I needed it?

Did I remember my intentions from last week?

Did I spend enough time being unplugged?

I am proud that I....

Notes:

WEEKLY CHECK-IN

My Intention for Next Week:

I would like to:

Experience…

Let go of…

Feel…

Learn to…

Stop…

I want more of…	I want less of…

The two most important days in your life are the day you were born and the day you find out why. (Mark Twain)

Date:	Mood/Happiness Scale (1-10): AM PM
I am grateful for:	

What is happening in my life today?

Was I of service?	Did I share how I was feeling?
I'm excited about:	Did I enrich my spiritual life?
What am I fearful of?	Do I owe an amend?
Did I struggle today?	Why?
Was I kind?	My plan for tomorrow:
Was I Hungry, Angry, Lonely or Tired?	

The task ahead of us is never as great as the Power behind us.
(Ralph Waldo Emerson)

Date:	Mood/Happiness Scale (1-10): AM PM
I am grateful for:	
What is happening in my life today?	
Was I of service?	Did I share how I was feeling?
I'm excited about:	Did I enrich my spiritual life?
What am I fearful of?	Do I owe an amend?
Did I struggle today?	Why?
Was I kind?	My plan for tomorrow:
Was I Hungry, Angry, Lonely or Tired?	

It's all an inside job.

Date:	Mood/Happiness Scale (1-10): AM PM

I am grateful for:

What is happening in my life today?

Was I of service?	Did I share how I was feeling?
I'm excited about:	Did I enrich my spiritual life?
What am I fearful of?	Do I owe an amend?
Did I struggle today?	Why?
Was I kind?	My plan for tomorrow:
Was I Hungry, Angry, Lonely or Tired?	

Do you want to be right or do you want to be happy?

Date:	Mood/Happiness Scale (1-10): AM PM
I am grateful for:	
What is happening in my life today?	
Was I of service?	Did I share how I was feeling?
I'm excited about:	Did I enrich my spiritual life?
What am I fearful of?	Do I owe an amend?
Did I struggle today?	Why?
Was I kind?	My plan for tomorrow:
Was I Hungry, Angry, Lonely or Tired?	

Each new day offers twenty-four hours of possibility and moves you forward on your path.

Date:	Mood/Happiness Scale (1-10): AM PM
I am grateful for:	
What is happening in my life today?	

Was I of service?	Did I share how I was feeling?
I'm excited about:	Did I enrich my spiritual life?
What am I fearful of?	Do I owe an amend?
Did I struggle today?	Why?
Was I kind?	My plan for tomorrow:
Was I Hungry, Angry, Lonely or Tired?	

Each day may not be good, but there is good in every day. (Alice Earle)

Date:	Mood/Happiness Scale (1-10): AM PM

I am grateful for:

What is happening in my life today?

Was I of service?	Did I share how I was feeling?
I'm excited about:	Did I enrich my spiritual life?
What am I fearful of?	Do I owe an amend?
Did I struggle today?	Why?
Was I kind?	My plan for tomorrow:
Was I Hungry, Angry, Lonely or Tired?	

The first step towards getting somewhere is to decide that you are not going to stay where you are.

Date:	Mood/Happiness Scale (1-10): AM PM

I am grateful for:

What is happening in my life today?

Was I of service?	Did I share how I was feeling?
I'm excited about:	Did I enrich my spiritual life?
What am I fearful of?	Do I owe an amend?
Did I struggle today?	Why?
Was I kind?	My plan for tomorrow:
Was I Hungry, Angry, Lonely or Tired?	

REVIEW OF LAST WEEK

How balanced was my time? (work/family/Me)	Did I get outside every day for fresh air?
Did I have the support I needed?	Did I ask for help when I needed it?

Did I remember my intentions from last week?

Did I spend enough time being unplugged?

I am proud that I....

Notes:

WEEKLY CHECK-IN

My Intention for Next Week:

I would like to:

Experience…

Let go of…

Feel…

Learn to…

Stop…

I want more of…	I want less of…

It's not about being the best, it's about being better than you were yesterday.

Date:	Mood/Happiness Scale (1-10): AM PM
I am grateful for:	
What is happening in my life today?	
Was I of service?	**Did I share how I was feeling?**
I'm excited about:	**Did I enrich my spiritual life?**
What am I fearful of?	**Do I owe an amend?**
Did I struggle today?	**Why?**
Was I kind?	**My plan for tomorrow:**
Was I Hungry, Angry, Lonely or Tired?	

The mind is slow in unlearning what it has been long in learning. (Seneca)

Date:	Mood/Happiness Scale (1-10): AM PM

I am grateful for:

What is happening in my life today?

Was I of service?	Did I share how I was feeling?
I'm excited about:	Did I enrich my spiritual life?
What am I fearful of?	Do I owe an amend?
Did I struggle today?	Why?
Was I kind?	My plan for tomorrow:
Was I Hungry, Angry, Lonely or Tired?	

*Be ready at any moment to sacrifice what you are
for what you could become. (Charles Dubois)*

Date:	Mood/Happiness Scale (1-10): AM　　　　　　　PM
I am grateful for:	
What is happening in my life today?	
Was I of service?	Did I share how I was feeling?
I'm excited about:	Did I enrich my spiritual life?
What am I fearful of?	Do I owe an amend?
Did I struggle today?	Why?
Was I kind?	My plan for tomorrow:
Was I Hungry, Angry, Lonely or Tired?	

When one is willing and eager, the gods join in. (Aeschylus)

Date:	Mood/Happiness Scale (1-10): AM PM
I am grateful for:	
What is happening in my life today?	
Was I of service?	Did I share how I was feeling?
I'm excited about:	Did I enrich my spiritual life?
What am I fearful of?	Do I owe an amend?
Did I struggle today?	Why?
Was I kind?	My plan for tomorrow:
Was I Hungry, Angry, Lonely or Tired?	

The real voyage of discovery consists not in seeing new landscapes, but in having new eyes. (Marcel Proust)

Date:	Mood/Happiness Scale (1-10): AM　　　　　　　PM

I am grateful for:

What is happening in my life today?

Was I of service?	Did I share how I was feeling?
I'm excited about:	Did I enrich my spiritual life?
What am I fearful of?	Do I owe an amend?
Did I struggle today?	Why?
Was I kind?	My plan for tomorrow:
Was I Hungry, Angry, Lonely or Tired?	

There is no way to happiness. Happiness is the way. (Thich Nhat Hanh)

Date:	Mood/Happiness Scale (1-10): AM PM
I am grateful for:	

What is happening in my life today?

Was I of service?	Did I share how I was feeling?
I'm excited about:	Did I enrich my spiritual life?
What am I fearful of?	Do I owe an amend?
Did I struggle today?	Why?
Was I kind?	My plan for tomorrow:
Was I Hungry, Angry, Lonely or Tired?	

Be the change you want to see in the world. (Mahatma Gandhi)

Date:	Mood/Happiness Scale (1-10): AM PM
I am grateful for:	

What is happening in my life today?

Was I of service?	Did I share how I was feeling?
I'm excited about:	Did I enrich my spiritual life?
What am I fearful of?	Do I owe an amend?
Did I struggle today?	Why?
Was I kind?	My plan for tomorrow:
Was I Hungry, Angry, Lonely or Tired?	

REVIEW OF LAST WEEK

How balanced was my time? (work/family/Me)	Did I get outside every day for fresh air?
Did I have the support I needed?	Did I ask for help when I needed it?

Did I remember my intentions from last week?

Did I spend enough time being unplugged?

I am proud that I....

Notes:

WEEKLY CHECK-IN

My Intention for Next Week:

I would like to:

Experience...

Let go of...

Feel...

Learn to...

Stop...

I want more of...	I want less of...

If the only prayer you ever say in your whole life is "thank you", that would suffice. (Meister Eckhart)

Date:	Mood/Happiness Scale (1-10): AM　　　　　　　PM
I am grateful for:	
What is happening in my life today?	

Was I of service?	Did I share how I was feeling?
I'm excited about:	Did I enrich my spiritual life?
What am I fearful of?	Do I owe an amend?
Did I struggle today?	Why?
Was I kind?	My plan for tomorrow:
Was I Hungry, Angry, Lonely or Tired?	

Believe in miracles, but do the footwork.

Date:	Mood/Happiness Scale (1-10): AM PM

I am grateful for:

What is happening in my life today?

Was I of service?	Did I share how I was feeling?
I'm excited about:	Did I enrich my spiritual life?
What am I fearful of?	Do I owe an amend?
Did I struggle today?	Why?
Was I kind?	My plan for tomorrow:
Was I Hungry, Angry, Lonely or Tired?	

Leave room—life's most treasured moments often come unannounced.

Date:	Mood/Happiness Scale (1-10): AM PM
I am grateful for:	

What is happening in my life today?

Was I of service?	Did I share how I was feeling?
I'm excited about:	Did I enrich my spiritual life?
What am I fearful of?	Do I owe an amend?
Did I struggle today?	Why?
Was I kind?	My plan for tomorrow:
Was I Hungry, Angry, Lonely or Tired?	

Be willing to accept a temporary inconvenience for a permanent improvement.

Date:	Mood/Happiness Scale (1-10): AM PM

I am grateful for:

What is happening in my life today?

Was I of service?	Did I share how I was feeling?
I'm excited about:	Did I enrich my spiritual life?
What am I fearful of?	Do I owe an amend?
Did I struggle today?	Why?
Was I kind?	My plan for tomorrow:
Was I Hungry, Angry, Lonely or Tired?	

Seek respect rather than popularity.

Date:	Mood/Happiness Scale (1-10): AM PM
I am grateful for:	
What is happening in my life today?	
Was I of service?	Did I share how I was feeling?
I'm excited about:	Did I enrich my spiritual life?
What am I fearful of?	Do I owe an amend?
Did I struggle today?	Why?
Was I kind?	My plan for tomorrow:
Was I Hungry, Angry, Lonely or Tired?	

Is what you're doing today getting you closer to where you want to be tomorrow?

Date:	Mood/Happiness Scale (1-10): AM PM
I am grateful for:	
What is happening in my life today?	
Was I of service?	Did I share how I was feeling?
I'm excited about:	Did I enrich my spiritual life?
What am I fearful of?	Do I owe an amend?
Did I struggle today?	Why?
Was I kind?	My plan for tomorrow:
Was I Hungry, Angry, Lonely or Tired?	

Belief is simply acceptance without proof.

Date:	Mood/Happiness Scale (1-10): AM PM
I am grateful for:	
What is happening in my life today?	
Was I of service?	Did I share how I was feeling?
I'm excited about:	Did I enrich my spiritual life?
What am I fearful of?	Do I owe an amend?
Did I struggle today?	Why?
Was I kind?	My plan for tomorrow:
Was I Hungry, Angry, Lonely or Tired?	

REVIEW OF LAST WEEK

How balanced was my time? (work/family/Me)	Did I get outside every day for fresh air?
Did I have the support I needed?	Did I ask for help when I needed it?

Did I remember my intentions from last week?

Did I spend enough time being unplugged?

I am proud that I....

Notes:

WEEKLY CHECK-IN

My Intention for Next Week:

I would like to:

Experience…

Let go of…

Feel…

Learn to…

Stop…

I want more of…	I want less of…

The only people with whom you should try to get even with are those who have helped you. (John E. Southard)

Date:	Mood/Happiness Scale (1-10): AM PM
I am grateful for:	
What is happening in my life today?	

Was I of service?	Did I share how I was feeling?
I'm excited about:	Did I enrich my spiritual life?
What am I fearful of?	Do I owe an amend?
Did I struggle today?	Why?
Was I kind?	My plan for tomorrow:
Was I Hungry, Angry, Lonely or Tired?	

Failure isn't being knocked down—it's staying down.

Date:	Mood/Happiness Scale (1-10): AM PM
I am grateful for:	

What is happening in my life today?

Was I of service?	Did I share how I was feeling?
I'm excited about:	Did I enrich my spiritual life?
What am I fearful of?	Do I owe an amend?
Did I struggle today?	Why?
Was I kind?	My plan for tomorrow:
Was I Hungry, Angry, Lonely or Tired?	

What do you dream of when no one is watching?

Date:	Mood/Happiness Scale (1-10): AM PM

I am grateful for:

What is happening in my life today?

Was I of service?	Did I share how I was feeling?
I'm excited about:	Did I enrich my spiritual life?
What am I fearful of?	Do I owe an amend?
Did I struggle today?	Why?
Was I kind?	My plan for tomorrow:
Was I Hungry, Angry, Lonely or Tired?	

The more we resist, the more stuck we become.

Date:	Mood/Happiness Scale (1-10): AM PM

I am grateful for:

What is happening in my life today?

Was I of service?	Did I share how I was feeling?
I'm excited about:	Did I enrich my spiritual life?
What am I fearful of?	Do I owe an amend?
Did I struggle today?	Why?
Was I kind?	My plan for tomorrow:
Was I Hungry, Angry, Lonely or Tired?	

Start each day with a sense of possibility.

Date:	Mood/Happiness Scale (1-10): AM PM
I am grateful for:	

What is happening in my life today?

Was I of service?	Did I share how I was feeling?
I'm excited about:	Did I enrich my spiritual life?
What am I fearful of?	Do I owe an amend?
Did I struggle today?	Why?
Was I kind?	My plan for tomorrow:
Was I Hungry, Angry, Lonely or Tired?	

The same boiling water that softens the potato hardens the egg. It's about what you're made of, not the circumstances. (Unknown)

Date:	Mood/Happiness Scale (1-10): AM PM

I am grateful for:

What is happening in my life today?

Was I of service?	Did I share how I was feeling?
I'm excited about:	Did I enrich my spiritual life?
What am I fearful of?	Do I owe an amend?
Did I struggle today?	Why?
Was I kind?	My plan for tomorrow:
Was I Hungry, Angry, Lonely or Tired?	

We know what we are but know not what we may be.
(William Shakespeare)

Date:	Mood/Happiness Scale (1-10): AM PM
I am grateful for:	

What is happening in my life today?

Was I of service?	Did I share how I was feeling?
I'm excited about:	Did I enrich my spiritual life?
What am I fearful of?	Do I owe an amend?
Did I struggle today?	Why?
Was I kind?	My plan for tomorrow:
Was I Hungry, Angry, Lonely or Tired?	

REVIEW OF LAST WEEK

How balanced was my time? (work/family/Me)	Did I get outside every day for fresh air?
Did I have the support I needed?	Did I ask for help when I needed it?

Did I remember my intentions from last week?

Did I spend enough time being unplugged?

I am proud that I....

Notes:

WEEKLY CHECK-IN

My Intention for Next Week:

I would like to:

Experience...

Let go of...

Feel...

Learn to...

Stop...

I want more of...	I want less of...

I care not so much what I am to others as what I am to myself.
(Michel Eyquem de Montaigne)

Date:	Mood/Happiness Scale (1-10): AM PM

I am grateful for:

What is happening in my life today?

Was I of service?	Did I share how I was feeling?
I'm excited about:	Did I enrich my spiritual life?
What am I fearful of?	Do I owe an amend?
Did I struggle today?	Why?
Was I kind?	My plan for tomorrow:
Was I Hungry, Angry, Lonely or Tired?	

We are what we do, not what we say we do.

Date:	Mood/Happiness Scale (1-10): AM PM
I am grateful for:	
What is happening in my life today?	
Was I of service?	Did I share how I was feeling?
I'm excited about:	Did I enrich my spiritual life?
What am I fearful of?	Do I owe an amend?
Did I struggle today?	Why?
Was I kind?	My plan for tomorrow:
Was I Hungry, Angry, Lonely or Tired?	

Let your faith be bigger than your fear.

Date:	Mood/Happiness Scale (1-10): AM PM
I am grateful for:	
What is happening in my life today?	
Was I of service?	Did I share how I was feeling?
I'm excited about:	Did I enrich my spiritual life?
What am I fearful of?	Do I owe an amend?
Did I struggle today?	Why?
Was I kind?	My plan for tomorrow:
Was I Hungry, Angry, Lonely or Tired?	

Do the next right thing.

Date:	Mood/Happiness Scale (1-10): AM PM

I am grateful for:

What is happening in my life today?

Was I of service?	Did I share how I was feeling?
I'm excited about:	Did I enrich my spiritual life?
What am I fearful of?	Do I owe an amend?
Did I struggle today?	Why?
Was I kind?	My plan for tomorrow:
Was I Hungry, Angry, Lonely or Tired?	

Don't complain about the things you're not willing to change.

| Date: | Mood/Happiness Scale (1-10): |
| | AM PM |

| I am grateful for: |
| |
| |
| |

| What is happening in my life today? |
| |

| Was I of service? | Did I share how I was feeling? |

| I'm excited about: | Did I enrich my spiritual life? |

| What am I fearful of? | Do I owe an amend? |

| Did I struggle today? | Why? |

| Was I kind? | My plan for tomorrow: |
| Was I Hungry, Angry, Lonely or Tired? | |

You are not here to figure out your life, you are here to create it.

Date:	Mood/Happiness Scale (1-10): AM PM

I am grateful for:

What is happening in my life today?

Was I of service?	Did I share how I was feeling?
I'm excited about:	Did I enrich my spiritual life?
What am I fearful of?	Do I owe an amend?
Did I struggle today?	Why?
Was I kind?	My plan for tomorrow:
Was I Hungry, Angry, Lonely or Tired?	

*Stop worrying about what can go wrong and
get excited about what can go right.*

Date:	Mood/Happiness Scale (1-10): AM PM

I am grateful for:

What is happening in my life today?

Was I of service?	Did I share how I was feeling?
I'm excited about:	Did I enrich my spiritual life?
What am I fearful of?	Do I owe an amend?
Did I struggle today?	Why?
Was I kind? Was I Hungry, Angry, Lonely or Tired?	My plan for tomorrow:

REVIEW OF LAST WEEK

How balanced was my time? (work/family/Me)	Did I get outside every day for fresh air?
Did I have the support I needed?	Did I ask for help when I needed it?

Did I remember my intentions from last week?

Did I spend enough time being unplugged?

I am proud that I....

Notes:

WEEKLY CHECK-IN

My Intention for Next Week:

I would like to:

Experience...

Let go of...

Feel...

Learn to...

Stop...

I want more of...	I want less of...

If there is no change, there is no change.

Date:	Mood/Happiness Scale (1-10): AM PM
I am grateful for:	

What is happening in my life today?

Was I of service?	**Did I share how I was feeling?**
I'm excited about:	**Did I enrich my spiritual life?**
What am I fearful of?	**Do I owe an amend?**
Did I struggle today?	**Why?**
Was I kind?	**My plan for tomorrow:**
Was I Hungry, Angry, Lonely or Tired?	

Life: It's the greatest journey you will ever be on.

Date:	Mood/Happiness Scale (1-10): AM PM

I am grateful for:

What is happening in my life today?

Was I of service?	Did I share how I was feeling?
I'm excited about:	Did I enrich my spiritual life?
What am I fearful of?	Do I owe an amend?
Did I struggle today?	Why?
Was I kind?	My plan for tomorrow:
Was I Hungry, Angry, Lonely or Tired?	

You are today where your thoughts have brought you; you will be tomorrow where your thoughts take you. (James Allen)

Date:	Mood/Happiness Scale (1-10): AM PM
I am grateful for:	
What is happening in my life today?	
Was I of service?	Did I share how I was feeling?
I'm excited about:	Did I enrich my spiritual life?
What am I fearful of?	Do I owe an amend?
Did I struggle today?	Why?
Was I kind?	My plan for tomorrow:
Was I Hungry, Angry, Lonely or Tired?	

Most people are about as happy as they make up their minds to be.
(Abraham Lincoln)

Date:	Mood/Happiness Scale (1-10): AM PM

I am grateful for:

What is happening in my life today?

Was I of service?	Did I share how I was feeling?
I'm excited about:	Did I enrich my spiritual life?
What am I fearful of?	Do I owe an amend?
Did I struggle today?	Why?
Was I kind?	My plan for tomorrow:
Was I Hungry, Angry, Lonely or Tired?	

The love of oneself is the beginning of a lifelong romance. (Oscar Wilde)

Date:	Mood/Happiness Scale (1-10): AM PM
I am grateful for:	
What is happening in my life today?	
Was I of service?	Did I share how I was feeling?
I'm excited about:	Did I enrich my spiritual life?
What am I fearful of?	Do I owe an amend?
Did I struggle today?	Why?
Was I kind?	My plan for tomorrow:
Was I Hungry, Angry, Lonely or Tired?	

To accomplish great things, we must not only act, but also dream, not only plan, but also believe. (Anatole France)

Date:	Mood/Happiness Scale (1-10): AM PM
I am grateful for:	
What is happening in my life today?	
Was I of service?	Did I share how I was feeling?
I'm excited about:	Did I enrich my spiritual life?
What am I fearful of?	Do I owe an amend?
Did I struggle today?	Why?
Was I kind?	My plan for tomorrow:
Was I Hungry, Angry, Lonely or Tired?	

Let yourself be silently drawn by the stronger pull of what you really love.
(Rumi)

Date:	Mood/Happiness Scale (1-10): AM PM
I am grateful for:	

What is happening in my life today?

Was I of service?	Did I share how I was feeling?
I'm excited about:	Did I enrich my spiritual life?
What am I fearful of?	Do I owe an amend?
Did I struggle today?	Why?
Was I kind?	My plan for tomorrow:
Was I Hungry, Angry, Lonely or Tired?	

REVIEW OF LAST WEEK

How balanced was my time? (work/family/Me)	Did I get outside every day for fresh air?
Did I have the support I needed?	Did I ask for help when I needed it?

Did I remember my intentions from last week?

Did I spend enough time being unplugged?

I am proud that I....

Notes:

WEEKLY CHECK-IN

My Intention for Next Week:

I would like to:

Experience…

Let go of…

Feel…

Learn to…

Stop…

I want more of…	I want less of…

Start by doing what is necessary; then do what's possible; and suddenly you are doing the impossible. (St. Francis of Assisi)

Date:	Mood/Happiness Scale (1-10): AM PM

I am grateful for:

What is happening in my life today?

Was I of service?	Did I share how I was feeling?
I'm excited about:	Did I enrich my spiritual life?
What am I fearful of?	Do I owe an amend?
Did I struggle today?	Why?
Was I kind?	My plan for tomorrow:
Was I Hungry, Angry, Lonely or Tired?	

Maybe it's about unbecoming everything that isn't really you, so you can be who you were meant to be in the first place. (Unknown)

Date:	Mood/Happiness Scale (1-10): AM　　　　　　　PM
I am grateful for:	
What is happening in my life today?	
Was I of service?	Did I share how I was feeling?
I'm excited about:	Did I enrich my spiritual life?
What am I fearful of?	Do I owe an amend?
Did I struggle today?	Why?
Was I kind?	My plan for tomorrow:
Was I Hungry, Angry, Lonely or Tired?	

Life is really simple, but we insist on making it complicated. (Confucius)

Date:	Mood/Happiness Scale (1-10): AM PM

I am grateful for:

What is happening in my life today?

Was I of service?	Did I share how I was feeling?
I'm excited about:	Did I enrich my spiritual life?
What am I fearful of?	Do I owe an amend?
Did I struggle today?	Why?
Was I kind?	My plan for tomorrow:
Was I Hungry, Angry, Lonely or Tired?	

Very little is needed to make a happy life; it is all within yourself, in your way of thinking. (Marcus Aurelius)

Date:	Mood/Happiness Scale (1-10): AM PM
I am grateful for:	
What is happening in my life today?	
Was I of service?	Did I share how I was feeling?
I'm excited about:	Did I enrich my spiritual life?
What am I fearful of?	Do I owe an amend?
Did I struggle today?	Why?
Was I kind?	My plan for tomorrow:
Was I Hungry, Angry, Lonely or Tired?	

Let your dreams be bigger than your fears, your actions louder than your words and your faith stronger than your feelings. (Unknown)

Date:	Mood/Happiness Scale (1-10): AM PM
I am grateful for:	
What is happening in my life today?	
Was I of service?	Did I share how I was feeling?
I'm excited about:	Did I enrich my spiritual life?
What am I fearful of?	Do I owe an amend?
Did I struggle today?	Why?
Was I kind?	My plan for tomorrow:
Was I Hungry, Angry, Lonely or Tired?	

I am only one, but I am one. I cannot do everything, but I can do something and I will not let what I cannot do interfere with what I can do. (Edward Everett Hale)

Date:	Mood/Happiness Scale (1-10): AM PM

I am grateful for:

What is happening in my life today?

Was I of service?	Did I share how I was feeling?
I'm excited about:	Did I enrich my spiritual life?
What am I fearful of?	Do I owe an amend?
Did I struggle today?	Why?
Was I kind?	My plan for tomorrow:
Was I Hungry, Angry, Lonely or Tired?	

Tension is who you think you should be. Relaxation is who you are.
(Chinese Proverb)

Date:	Mood/Happiness Scale (1-10): AM PM
I am grateful for:	

What is happening in my life today?

Was I of service?	Did I share how I was feeling?
I'm excited about:	Did I enrich my spiritual life?
What am I fearful of?	Do I owe an amend?
Did I struggle today?	Why?
Was I kind?	My plan for tomorrow:
Was I Hungry, Angry, Lonely or Tired?	

REVIEW OF LAST WEEK

How balanced was my time? (work/family/Me)	Did I get outside every day for fresh air?
Did I have the support I needed?	Did I ask for help when I needed it?

Did I remember my intentions from last week?

Did I spend enough time being unplugged?

I am proud that I....

Notes:

WEEKLY CHECK-IN

My Intention for Next Week:

I would like to:

Experience…

Let go of…

Feel…

Learn to…

Stop…

I want more of…	I want less of…

Go confidently in the direction of your dreams and live the life you have imagined. (Henry David Thoreau)

Date:	Mood/Happiness Scale (1-10): AM PM
I am grateful for:	
What is happening in my life today?	
Was I of service?	Did I share how I was feeling?
I'm excited about:	Did I enrich my spiritual life?
What am I fearful of?	Do I owe an amend?
Did I struggle today?	Why?
Was I kind?	My plan for tomorrow:
Was I Hungry, Angry, Lonely or Tired?	

You yourself, as much as anybody in the entire universe deserve your love and affection. (Buddha)

Date:	Mood/Happiness Scale (1-10): AM　　　　　　　　PM
I am grateful for:	
What is happening in my life today?	
Was I of service?	Did I share how I was feeling?
I'm excited about:	Did I enrich my spiritual life?
What am I fearful of?	Do I owe an amend?
Did I struggle today?	Why?
Was I kind?	My plan for tomorrow:
Was I Hungry, Angry, Lonely or Tired?	

Habit is a cable; we weave a thread of it each day, and at last we cannot break it. (Horace Mann)

Date:	Mood/Happiness Scale (1-10): AM PM

I am grateful for:

What is happening in my life today?

Was I of service?	Did I share how I was feeling?
I'm excited about:	Did I enrich my spiritual life?
What am I fearful of?	Do I owe an amend?
Did I struggle today?	Why?
Was I kind?	My plan for tomorrow:
Was I Hungry, Angry, Lonely or Tired?	

If a man wants his dreams to come true, he must wake them up. (Unknown)

Date:	Mood/Happiness Scale (1-10): AM　　　　　　　　PM
I am grateful for:	
What is happening in my life today?	
Was I of service?	Did I share how I was feeling?
I'm excited about:	Did I enrich my spiritual life?
What am I fearful of?	Do I owe an amend?
Did I struggle today?	Why?
Was I kind?	My plan for tomorrow:
Was I Hungry, Angry, Lonely or Tired?	

A comfort zone is a beautiful place, but nothing ever grows there.

Date:	Mood/Happiness Scale (1-10): AM PM
I am grateful for:	

What is happening in my life today?

Was I of service?	Did I share how I was feeling?
I'm excited about:	Did I enrich my spiritual life?
What am I fearful of?	Do I owe an amend?
Did I struggle today?	Why?
Was I kind?	My plan for tomorrow:
Was I Hungry, Angry, Lonely or Tired?	

There is only one way to happiness and that is to cease worrying about things which are beyond the power of our will. (Epictetus)

Date:	Mood/Happiness Scale (1-10): AM PM

I am grateful for:

What is happening in my life today?

Was I of service?	Did I share how I was feeling?
I'm excited about:	Did I enrich my spiritual life?
What am I fearful of?	Do I owe an amend?
Did I struggle today?	Why?
Was I kind? Was I Hungry, Angry, Lonely or Tired?	My plan for tomorrow:

True happiness is...to enjoy the present, without anxious dependence upon the future. (Lucius Annaeus Seneca)

Date:	Mood/Happiness Scale (1-10): AM　　　　　　　　PM

I am grateful for:

What is happening in my life today?

Was I of service?	Did I share how I was feeling?
I'm excited about:	Did I enrich my spiritual life?
What am I fearful of?	Do I owe an amend?
Did I struggle today?	Why?
Was I kind?	My plan for tomorrow:
Was I Hungry, Angry, Lonely or Tired?	

REVIEW OF LAST WEEK

How balanced was my time? (work/family/Me)	Did I get outside every day for fresh air?
Did I have the support I needed?	Did I ask for help when I needed it?

Did I remember my intentions from last week?

Did I spend enough time being unplugged?

I am proud that I....

Notes:

New Contact Information

Contact Information:

Name: _____

Phone #: _____

e-mail: _____

Address: _____

_____

Birthday: _____

Met: _____

Name: _____

Phone #: _____

e-mail: _____

Address: _____

_____

Birthday: _____

Met: _____

Contact Information:

Name: _____

Phone #: _____

e-mail: _____

Address: _____

_____

Birthday: _____

Met: _____

Name: _____

Phone #: _____

e-mail: _____

Address: _____

_____

Birthday: _____

Met: _____

Contact Information:

Name: _____

Phone #: _____

e-mail: _____

Address: _____

_____

Birthday: _____

Met: _____

Name: _____

Phone #: _____

e-mail: _____

Address: _____

_____

Birthday: _____

Met: _____

Contact Information:

Name: _____

Phone #: _____

e-mail: _____

Address: _____

_____

Birthday: _____

Met: _____

Name: _____

Phone #: _____

e-mail: _____

Address: _____

_____

Birthday: _____

Met: _____

Contact Information:

Name: _____

Phone #: _____

e-mail: _____

Address: _____

_____

Birthday: _____

Met: _____

Name: _____

Phone #: _____

e-mail: _____

Address: _____

_____

Birthday: _____

Met: _____

Contact Information:

Name: _____

Phone #: _____

e-mail: _____

Address: _____

_____

Birthday: _____

Met: _____

Name: _____

Phone #: _____

e-mail: _____

Address: _____

_____

Birthday: _____

Met: _____

Contact Information:

Name: _____

Phone #: _____

e-mail: _____

Address: _____

_____

Birthday: _____

Met: _____

Name: _____

Phone #: _____

e-mail: _____

Address: _____

_____

Birthday: _____

Met: _____

Contact Information:

Name: _____

Phone #: _____

e-mail: _____

Address: _____

_____

Birthday: _____

Met: _____

Name: _____

Phone #: _____

e-mail: _____

Address: _____

_____

Birthday: _____

Met: _____

Contact Information:

Name: _____

Phone #: _____

e-mail: _____

Address: _____

_____

Birthday: _____

Met: _____

Name: _____

Phone #: _____

e-mail: _____

Address: _____

_____

Birthday: _____

Met: _____

Contact Information:

Name: _____

Phone #: _____

e-mail: _____

Address: _____

_____

Birthday: _____

Met: _____

Name: _____

Phone #: _____

e-mail: _____

Address: _____

_____

Birthday: _____

Met: _____

Made in the USA
Charleston, SC
20 February 2016